WOODS BRANCH
GROSSE POINTE PUBLIC LIBRARY
GROSSE POINTE, MI 48236

George Did It

BY
SUZANNE
TRIPP JURMAIN

★

ILLUSTRATED BY
LARRY DAY

DUTTON
CHILDREN'S BOOKS

DUTTON CHILDREN'S BOOKS
A division of Penguin Young Readers Group

Published by the Penguin Group

Penguin Group (USA) Inc., 375 Hudson Street, New York, New York 10014, U.S.A. • Penguin Group (Canada), 10 Alcorn Avenue, Toronto, Ontario, Canada M4V 3B2 (a division of Pearson Penguin Canada Inc.) • Penguin Books Ltd, 80 Strand, London WC2R 0RL, England • Penguin Ireland, 25 St Stephen's Green, Dublin 2, Ireland (a division of Penguin Books Ltd) • Penguin Group (Australia), 250 Camberwell Road, Camberwell, Victoria 3124, Australia (a division of Pearson Australia Group Pty Ltd) • Penguin Books India Pvt Ltd, 11 Community Centre, Panchsheel Park, New Delhi—110 017, India • Penguin Group (NZ), Cnr Airborne and Rosedale Roads, Albany, Auckland 1310, New Zealand (a division of Pearson New Zealand Ltd) • Penguin Books (South Africa) (Pty) Ltd, 24 Sturdee Avenue, Rosebank, Johannesburg 2196, South Africa • Penguin Books Ltd, Registered Offices: 80 Strand, London WC2R 0RL, England

Text copyright © 2006 by Suzanne Tripp Jurmain / Illustrations copyright © 2006 by Larry Day • All rights reserved.

LIBRARY OF CONGRESS CATALOGING-IN-PUBLICATION DATA

Jurmain, Suzanne.

George did it/by Suzanne Tripp Jurmain; illustrated by Larry Day.—1st ed.

p. cm.

Includes bibliographical references.

ISBN 0-525-47560-5

1. Washington, George, 1732-1799—Juvenile literature. 2. Presidents—United States—Biography—Juvenile literature. I. Day, Larry, 1956- II. Title. • E312.66.J87 2006 • 973.4'1'092—dc22 2004025068

Published in the United States by Dutton Children's Books, a division of Penguin Young Readers Group
345 Hudson Street, New York, New York 10014 • www.penguin.com/youngreaders

Designed by Richard Amari

Manufactured in China • First Edition

1 3 5 7 9 10 8 6 4 2

★ ★ ★ ★ ★ SELECTED BIBLIOGRAPHY ★ ★ ★ ★ ★

Baker, William Spohn, ed. *Washington After the Revolution, MDCCLXXXIV–MDCCXCIX.* Philadelphia: J.B. Lippincott, 1898.

Bowling, Kenneth, and Helen Veit, eds. *Documentary History of the First Federal Congress of the United States of America, 4 March 1789–3 March 1791.* Vol. IX. *The Diary of William Maclay and Other Notes on Senate Debates.* Baltimore: Johns Hopkins University Press, 1988.

Burrows, Edwin G., and Mike Wallace. *Gotham: A History of New York City to 1898.* New York: Oxford University Press, 1999.

Custis, George Washington Parke. *Recollections and Private Memoirs of Washington by His Adopted Son.* New York: Derby and Jackson, 1860.

Fitzpatrick, John C., ed. *The Writings of George Washington from the Original Manuscript Sources, 1745–1799.* Vol. 30. June 20, 1788–January 1790. The United States George Washington Bicentennial Commission. Washington, D.C.: U.S. Government Printing Office, 1939.

Flexner, James Thomas. *George Washington and the New Nation (1783–1793).* Boston: Little, Brown, 1970.

———. *George Washington in the American Revolution (1775–1783).* Boston: Little, Brown, 1968.

———. *Washington: The Indispensable Man.* Boston: Little, Brown, 1974.

Harwell, Richard. *Washington: An Abridgement in One Volume of the Seven-Volume* George Washington *by Douglas Southall Freeman.* New York: Scribner's, 1968.

Schechter, Stephen L., and Richard B. Bernstein, eds. *Well Begun: Chronicles of the Early National Period.* Albany, N.Y.: New York State Commission on the Bicentennial of the United States Constitution, 1989.

Sellers, Charles Coleman. *Charles Willson Peale.* Vol. I. Philadelphia: The American Philosophical Society, 1947.

★ ★ ★ ★ ★ ★ ★ ★ ★ ★ ★ ★ ★

For David—the best of brothers
S.T.J.

For my friend, Pat Wroclawski, the quintessential children's bookseller
L.D.

Are presidents funny?

Some are. President George H. W. Bush sometimes wouldn't eat his vegetables because he didn't like broccoli. President John Quincy Adams once had to sit on the banks of the Potomac River in his underwear after his boat sank. Even George Washington had his silly moments. Tall George sometimes didn't pay attention to his short wife unless she pulled on his buttons.

Of course, George was also smart enough to be one of the best U.S. presidents and popular enough to be in office for eight long years.

And thanks to all the history books listed on the opposite page, we know a lot of facts about our first president. We know that George was sensible enough to hate wearing tight pants. We know he was big enough to need size 13 shoes. We know he was good-humored enough to laugh out loud when one of his hunting dogs stole a whole ham from the kitchen. And we also know another true and funny story about George Washington—which you can read if you turn to the very next page of this book.

In 1789, almost everyone in the country wanted George Washington to be the first president of the United States of America. Everyone—except George.

George was fifty-seven years old, and he wanted to stay home in Virginia to be with his wife, tend his farm, fix his house, and go foxhunting with his dogs.

For fourteen years, George hadn't had time for that. He'd been too busy. He was busy because Americans trusted George. They knew he was honest and dependable. So whenever a big, important job had to be done, Americans asked George to do it.

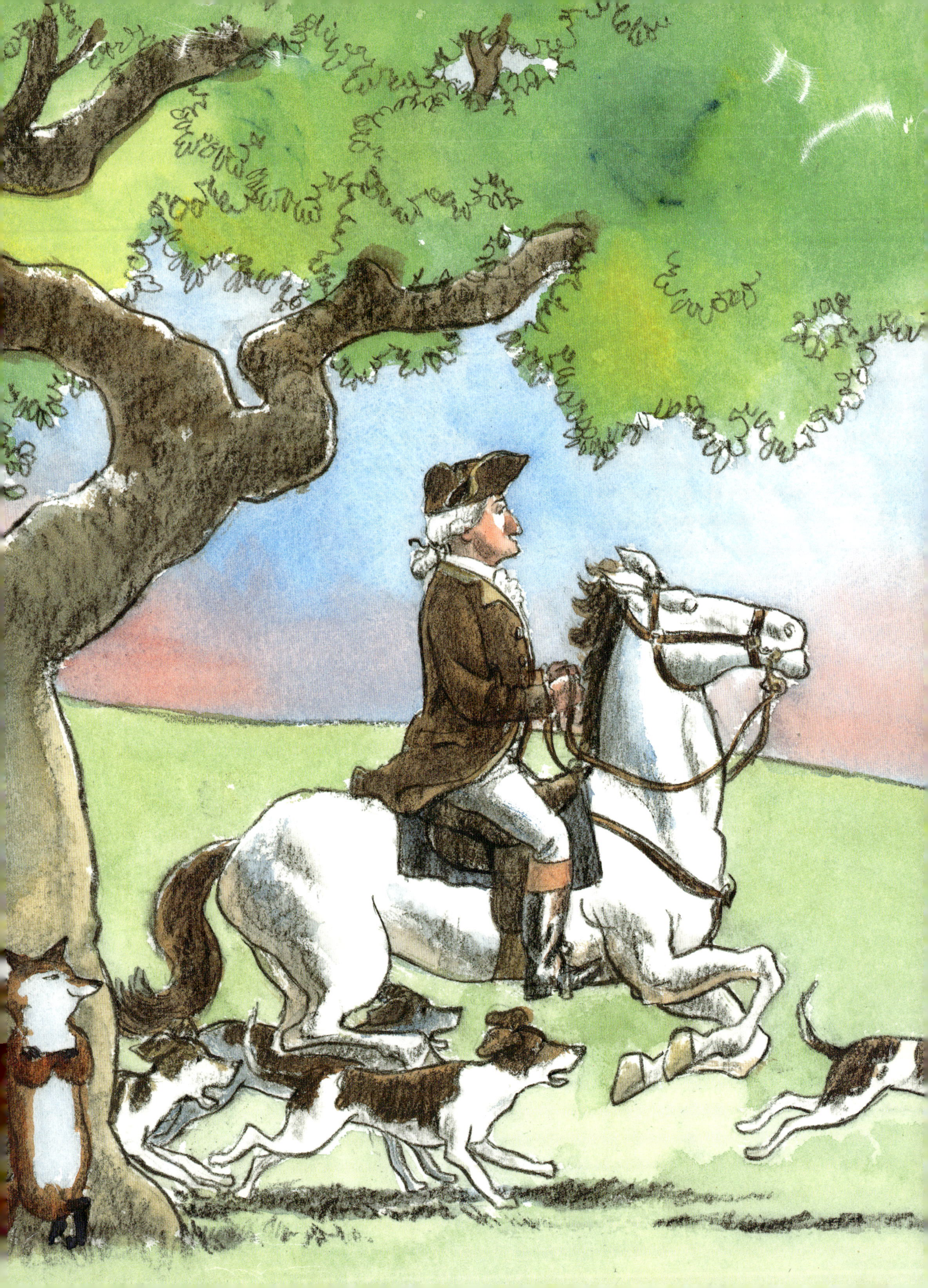

Back in 1775, when the thirteen American colonies were mad at the British king for making them pay unfair taxes, they asked George to be commander-in-chief of the brand-new Colonial army. It was hard to make soldiers out of tradesmen, shopkeepers, and farmers. But George did it.

Then, when war broke out, Americans asked George and his soldiers to fight the mighty British army so that the thirteen colonies could be free. That took almost eight years. But George did it.

After the war, when the country needed a good, strong government because the thirteen new American states all had different laws, different money, and different ideas, Americans asked George to help write the Constitution. It was hard to design a new government that would help all thirteen states to cooperate and unite into one big new nation. But George did it.

But when Americans asked George to be the first president of the brand-new United States of America, George said, NO, THANK YOU!

Being president was the biggest, most important job of all. And George absolutely, positively did not want to do it.

He was too old for the job, he told a friend. Too tired.

He didn't want to live in New York City (which Congress had chosen as the first capital of the United States).

And there was another reason—a big reason. Just thinking about being president made George NERVOUS.

Americans were counting on the first president to make sure the United States got off to a good start. They were counting on him to make sure the thirteen states stuck together. They were depending on him to manage the new government, approve the laws, appoint the judges, command the troops, take charge of the nation's money, and make friends with foreign countries. But what if George didn't do all those things? What if he couldn't? What if he didn't know how? There were so many *what ifs.* They buzzed around George's head like flies around a cherry pie. Nothing in his whole life, George said, filled him with "greater anxiety" than the thought of being president.

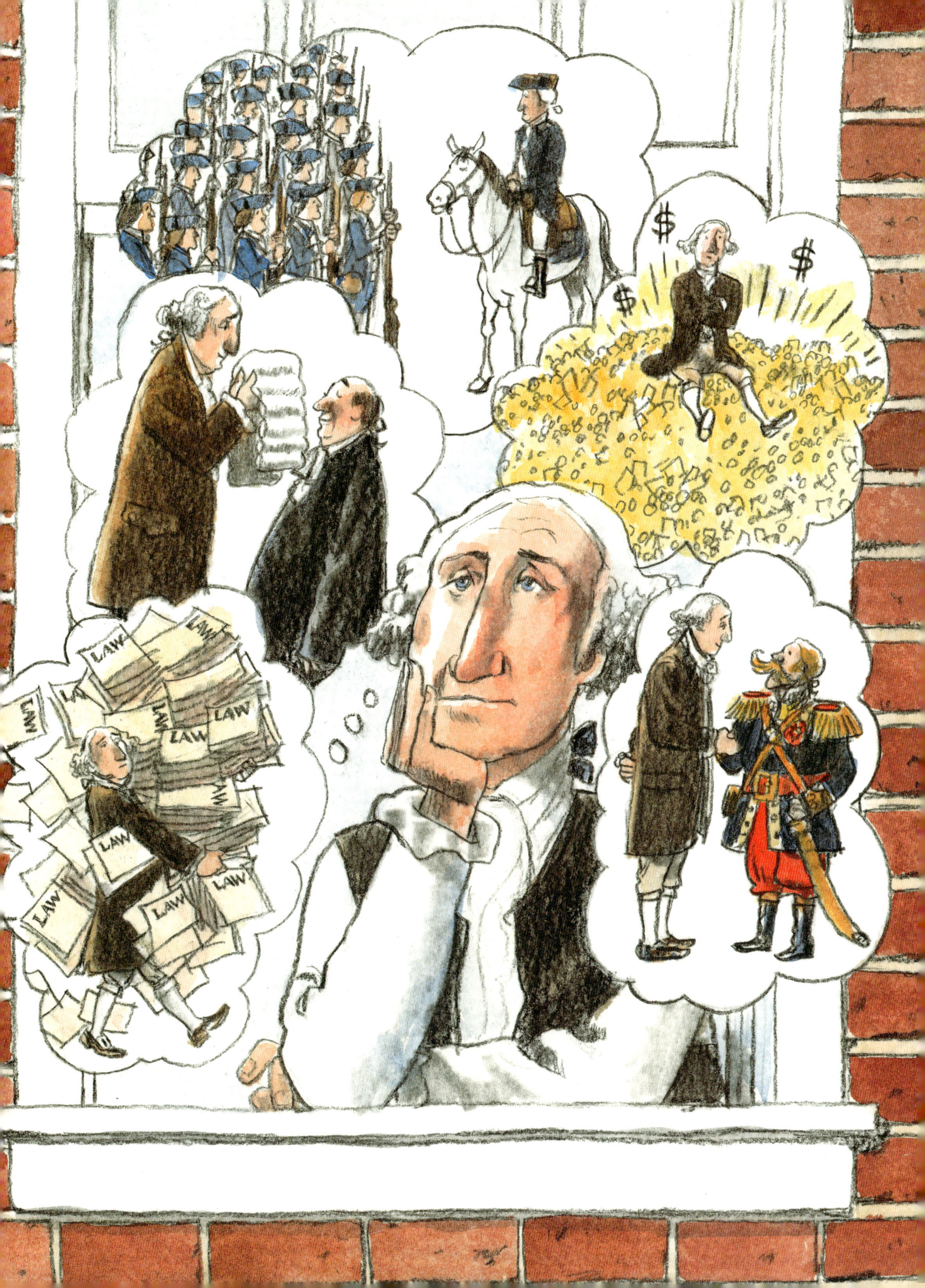
$
$
$
LAW
LAW
LAW
LAW
LAW
LAW
LAW
LAW
LAW
LAW

But, except for his wife, Martha, no one seemed to care how George felt.

Newspapers said George ought to be president. Friends like Thomas Jefferson (who wrote the Declaration of Independence) and Alexander Hamilton (who fought alongside George during the war) begged him to take the job. Some Americans said they'd be willing to support the new U.S. government *only* if George was elected.

So many people wanted George to be president that George finally said he'd take the job—if Americans thought it was "absolutely necessary."
They did.

CANDIDATES
GEORGE WASHINGTON
ALL OTHERS
GEORGE WASHINGTON!

When the United States held its first presidential election on February 4, 1789, George was the only candidate.

Two months later, when Congress officially counted the votes, George got every one.

Naturally, everyone was delighted. Everyone—except George. He said he felt like a criminal who was "going to...his execution."

But George couldn't waste time thinking about things like that. He was too busy. First, he went to say good-bye to his mother.

Then he made sure that his nephew knew how to take care of the farm while George was running the country.

After that, George had to write the speech for his inauguration (or swearing-in ceremony), which was to be held on April 30. And of course, in between, George and Martha had to rush around getting ready. Martha wasn't planning to go to New York until after the inauguration, but she had to help George. He had bags to pack, bills to pay, letters to write, and one big problem to solve.

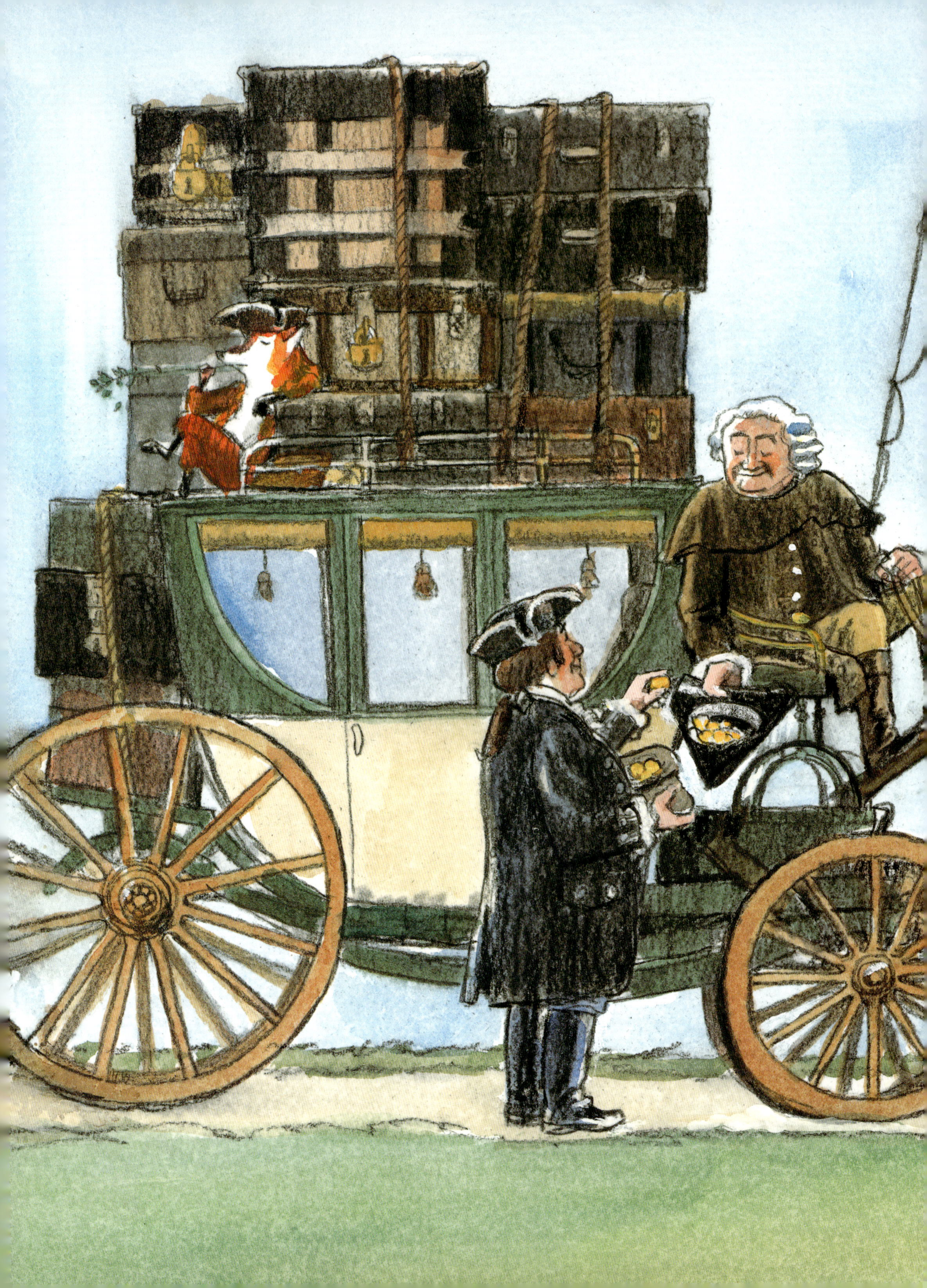

George had to get to New York to be president, but he didn't have enough money to pay for the eight-day trip. It cost so much to run his house and farm that George was short of cash. So he wrote to a neighbor. *Please, could I borrow one hundred pounds?* he asked. Luckily, the neighbor said yes.

On April 16, George kissed Martha good-bye and left, feeling "anxious" and "oppressed."

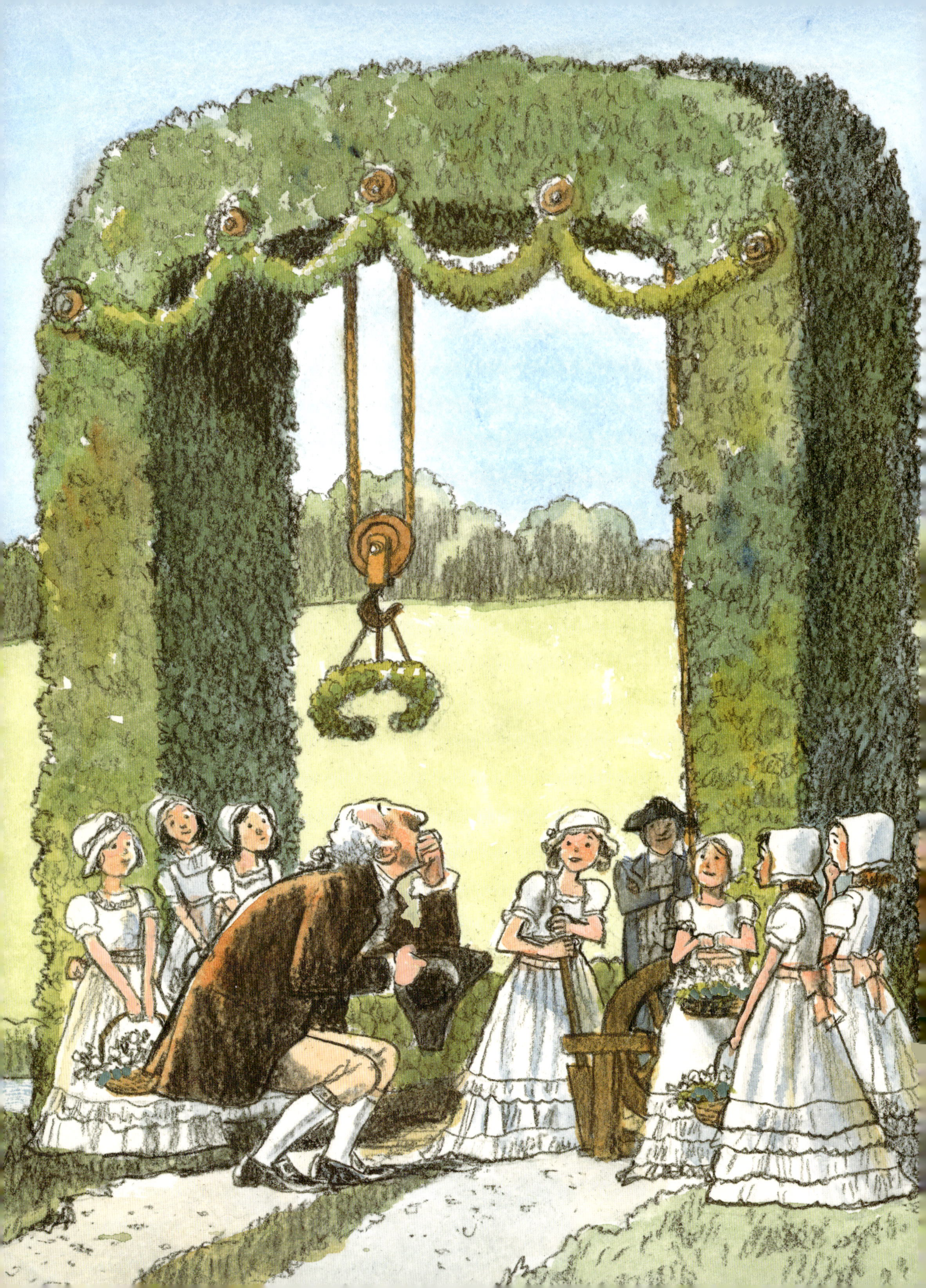

But everyone else was happy.

As George's coach rolled down the roads, crowds cheered. Bands played. Bells bonged. Everybody wanted to throw a party for George.

In Alexandria, Virginia, friends asked him to dinner. In Baltimore, there was a banquet. Philadelphia had fireworks, a banquet, and a parade. They even made George stand under a machine that dropped a hero's laurel wreath on his head. George was probably too embarrassed to wear the wreath, but he wanted to be polite. So he kissed the girl who operated the machinery.

At night he tried to stop worrying about being president, but it was hard to get to sleep. Sometimes the parties went on so long that George had to stay up until 10:00 P.M.—a whole hour past his usual bedtime. Yet no matter how late he stayed up or how much he worried, George always hopped out of bed at 4:00 A.M.,

jumped in his coach, and continued his journey to New York.
He knew the United States couldn't start its new government until he reached the city, so he tried to hurry. He begged people not to make a fuss. "Please, no reception when I arrive," he said. But the parties just kept getting bigger.

When George sailed from New Jersey to New York, a big parade of boats sailed with him. Bands played. Banners waved. Even the porpoises in New York Bay got into the act. They leaped and swam around George's barge.

One parade boat carried a group of singers. Another carried two orangutans. The singers sang:

*"Joy to our native land!…
For Washington's at hand…"*

The orangutans didn't sing anything, but the forts and warships in New York Harbor fired so many thirteen-gun salutes in George's honor that it sounded almost like a battle.

On shore there were more people. More hurrahs. And every time the crowd cheered, George felt NERVOUS.

He later wrote in his diary: *I greatly [fear]...my countrymen will expect too much of me.*

In New York, senators and congressmen, advisers and dignitaries came to George's house before breakfast, and they kept coming until he sat down to dinner. No one had ever started a brand-new government in a brand-new country before. So, naturally, there were lots of problems to discuss.

Some had to do with the Constitution. Many people wanted to add a special section called a Bill of Rights to protect important liberties, like the right to speak freely without fear of what the government might think, the right to choose a religion without fear of what the neighbors might think, and the right to be tried by a jury of ordinary citizens.

Another pressing problem was what to call the new president. Some of George's old friends called him "The General." His wife, Martha, sometimes called him her "old man." But what should other people call him? They couldn't just say "George." Not on formal occasions.

Everyone agreed that the new president needed a title. But what?

Most members of Congress thought it would be fine to say "President." Others thought that was too plain. They wanted to call George "His Elective Highness," "His Majesty," or maybe even "His Exalted High Mightiness, the President of the United States." Vice President John Adams agreed. He said other nations would "despise" the United States if the president didn't have a fancy title.

But other senators and congressmen pointed out that the Constitution specifically said that NO royal titles "shall be granted by the United States." That was final. So everyone settled on "President."

That suited George. He didn't want anyone to think he was trying to be a king.

His Majesty
The King
President
His Elective Highness
His Exalted High Mightiness, the President of the United States
The Supreme Preeminent Commander of Greatness

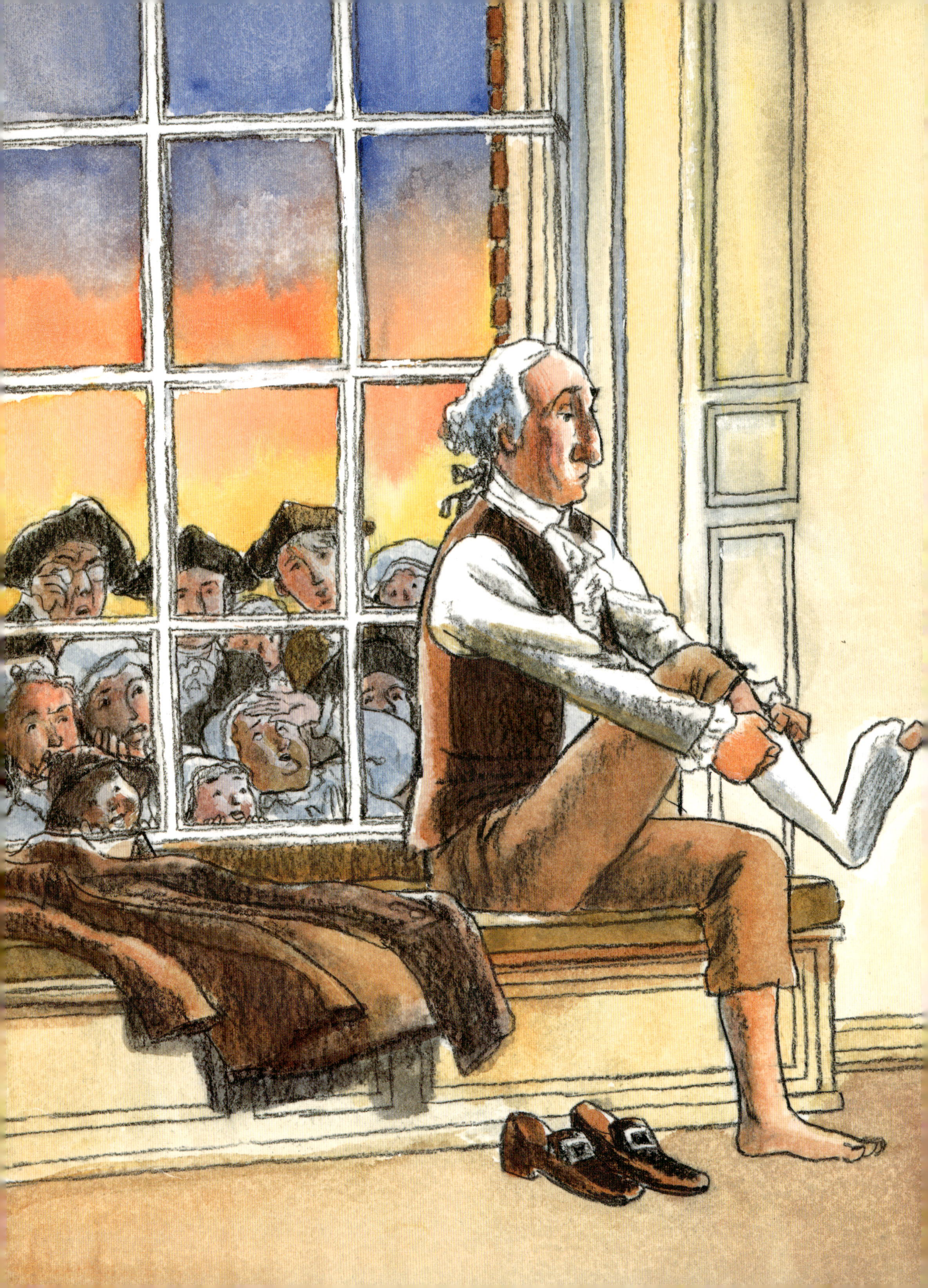

Of course, there were lots of other things that the new country had to worry about, and everybody was so busy discussing and arguing and visiting that time flew by. Then, all of a sudden, it was April 30—Inauguration Day.

That morning, soldiers woke the city at sunrise by firing off a thirteen-gun salute to George. Then almost everyone rushed down to Wall Street to get a good view of the swearing-in ceremony at Federal Hall.

George rushed around, too. He put on his best white silk stockings, his shoes with the shiny silver buckles, and, of course, his inauguration suit.

It was brown—because George liked brown suits. It was also very plain. That was important. George wanted Americans to know that the president was a plain, ordinary citizen like everybody else.

George was ready on time. Congress wasn't.

Inside Federal Hall, members of Congress were arguing. Should they stand when George gave his speech? Or sit? It took so long to decide that the senators in charge of bringing George to the inauguration picked up the new president a whole hour late for the ceremony.

Still, George didn't waste time. At Federal Hall he stepped right out on the balcony to swear his oath on the most important book Congress could think of—the Bible.

But where *was* the Bible?

Congress had forgotten to bring one. So everybody had to wait while a messenger borrowed a copy.

Finally, the chancellor of the State of New York read the oath. George put his big hand on the book. "I do solemnly swear that I will faithfully execute the Office of President of the United States, and will, to the best of my ability, preserve, protect, and defend the Constitution of the United States," he repeated. Then he kissed the Bible. "So help me, God," he added.

"Long live George Washington!" shouted the chancellor, and everybody cheered. Then it was time for George to make his speech.

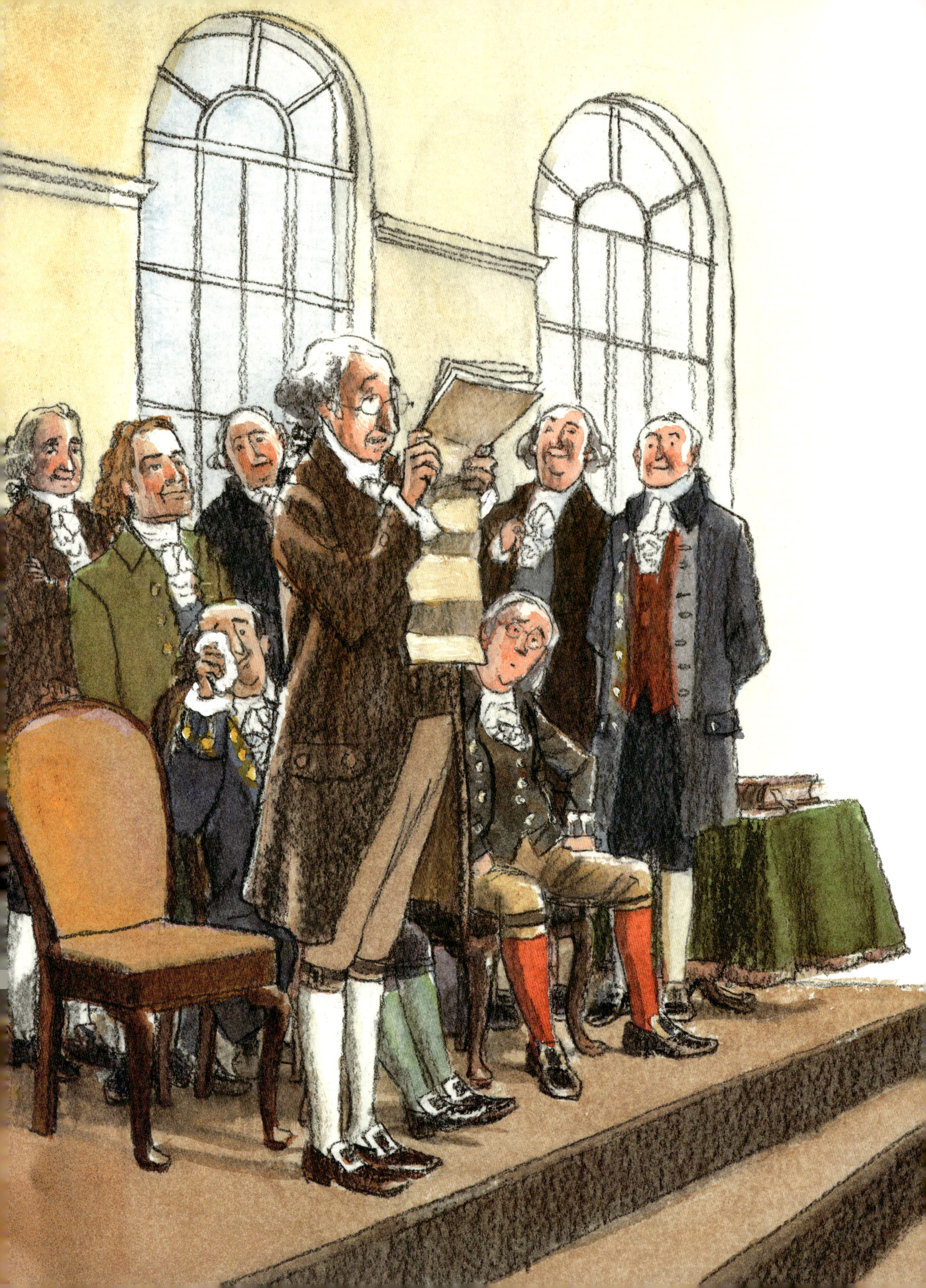

It was the biggest, most important speech he'd ever made, so, naturally, George was NERVOUS. His hands shook. His voice trembled. He quivered all over like a six-foot custard. But his message was clear. He asked Congress to work together and behave honorably. He asked them to add a Bill of Rights to the Constitution to protect the freedom of all Americans. And he asked God to bless the "liberties and happiness of the People of the United States."

He spoke for only twenty minutes. But at the end, George Washington looked tired. He'd tried to make a good speech, but still some people grumbled. One senator was shocked because George read the words and never took his "eyes from the paper." He couldn't understand how a brave general like George could be scared of making one little bitty speech.

Others thought the speech was moving and powerful. And Vice President John Adams was so overcome that he cried. Nobody knows how George felt. Probably he was just glad the speech was over.

But the inaugural celebration was just beginning.

First, George and the other dignitaries attended a special service at nearby St. Paul's Church. Then they watched fireworks and went to a grand party. Bands played, and so many New Yorkers came out to celebrate that George's coach couldn't roll through the crowded streets. That didn't bother George. He just walked to his house like everybody else.

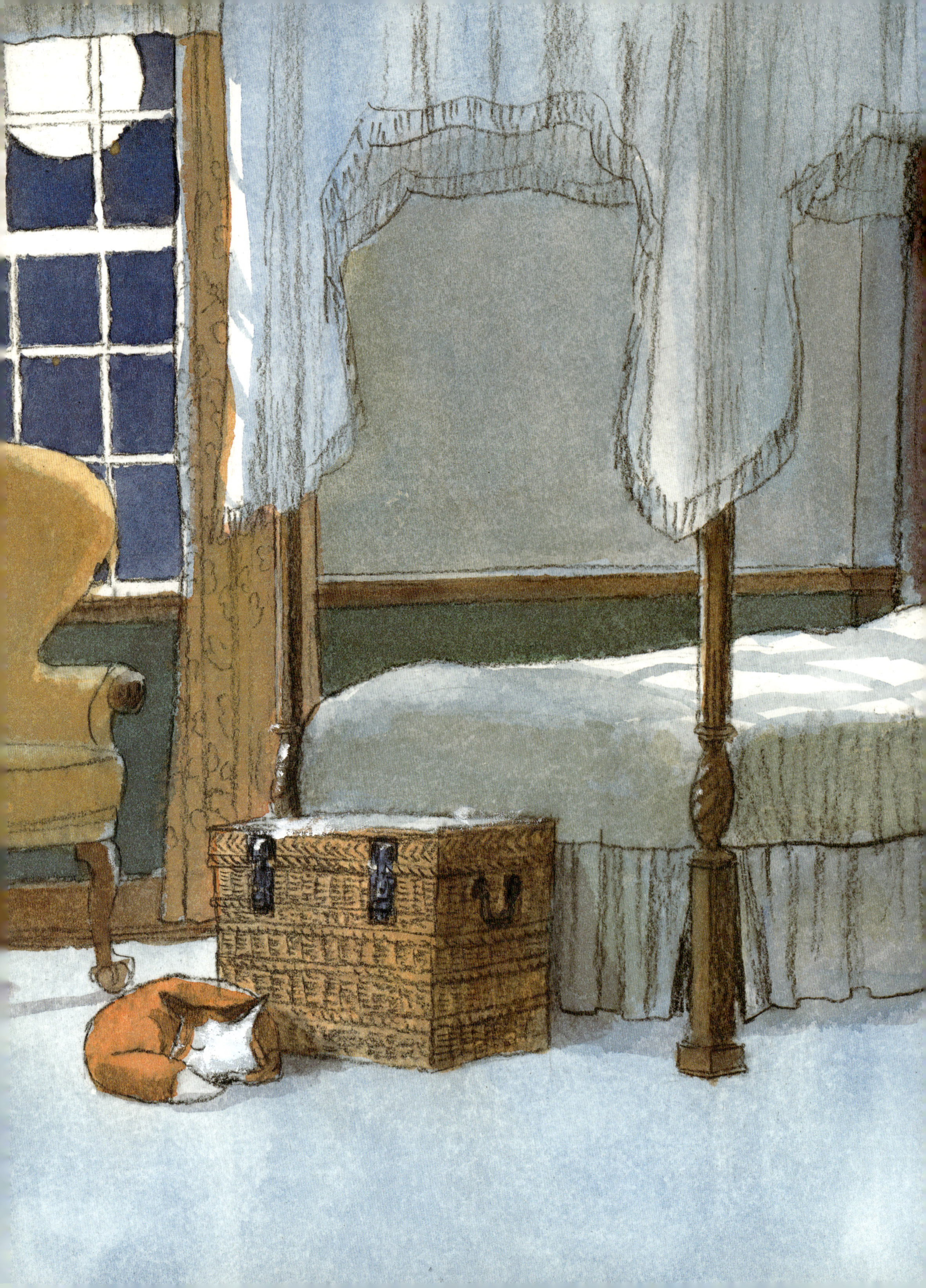

It had been a big day. At home, George blew out the candle and went to bed. He was still nervous about being president. But he didn't have time to think about that now. There was a big, important job to do.

And the very next morning…

George did it.